Let's Remember....

when TEXAS

BELONGED TO

MEXICO

Written and illustrated by Betsy Warren

1982 • HENDRICK-LONG PUBLISHING COMPANY • DALLAS

CONTENTS

ISBN 0-937460-07-9

1982 copyright © by Hendrick-Long, Dallas, Texas

MEXICO—A NEW COUNTRY . . . 1821

Mexico had belonged to Spain for more than 300 years. It became free from Spanish rule in the year 1821. Since Texas was a part of Mexico at that time, it was ruled by the new Mexican leaders. In the capital, Mexico City, they were busy making laws for the new country.

SETTLERS *from the* UNITED STATES
STEPHEN F. AUSTIN—1821

In 1821, Stephen F. Austin came to Texas. He brought 300 families from the United States to build homes and farms in East Texas. These settlers wanted to be sure that the Mexican rulers would let them own land in Texas. They also hoped that more families from the United States would be allowed to come. The settlers asked Stephen Austin to go to Mexico City to talk to the rulers about the things they wanted.

Stephen Austin rode 1200 miles to Mexico City. When he arrived, the rulers were too busy to see him.

Mr. Austin waited for a whole year. He had to sell his watch and borrow money to live. However, he spent his time learning the Spanish language. He also made many friends among the Mexican people. They liked and trusted him.

At last, the rulers in Mexico City listened to Stephen Austin.
They gave him permission to bring more people from the
United States in to East Texas. They promised to give land to
the settlers if they would obey Mexican laws and help fight the
Indians.

Stephen Austin hurried back to Texas to tell his friends the
news.

The settlers were glad to see Mr. Austin because they needed his help. They had run out of food and had no seeds to plant crops. Indians had stolen their cows and horses. Many families had left and gone back to the United States. Everyone was discouraged.

Mr. Austin had brought a large supply of seeds, tools, and gunpowder from San Antonio. He gave them to the settlers and helped them start their farms again. He met with the Indians and made peace with them. The settlers were greatly encouraged by the strong leadership of Stephen F. Austin.

BARON von BASTROP

More and more people from the United States came to Austin's colony. Each family was given 4428 acres of land for ranching, and 177 acres for farming. The colony grew so fast that Stephen Austin needed help in running it. He appointed Baron von Bastrop to help him survey (measure) the land for the new settlers. When the land was surveyed, each family knew exactly where its farm stood.

9

San Felipe

The FIRST ANGLO SETTLEMENT

By the year 1824, many cabins had been built on land close to the Brazos River. Farms near the settlement were doing well. The people voted to name their village "San Felipe de Austin". It was the first town in Texas to be built by Anglos (white-skinned, English-speaking people) from the United States.

10

By 1830, 4000 people lived in San Felipe. The town had houses, stores, a school for boys, a newspaper, and a ferry boat to carry people and wagons over the Brazos River.

Mr. Austin and Baron von Bastrop surveyed more land which had been granted by the Mexican rulers. A part of the land grant was near the coast. Another part spread as far west as the Colorado River where the city of Austin now stands.

OTHER LAND GRANTS

The Mexican rulers also gave large grants of land to other men who built colonies. Sterling Robertson and Green DeWitt brought people from the United States to establish homes near the Austin Colony.

Martin de León brought families from Mexico. They started large cattle ranches and built the town of Victoria.

Sometimes the colonists argued with each other about who owned the land. However, new families continued to come from the United States. Many of them brought slaves and built large cotton and rice plantations in Central and East Texas.

HOW THE SETTLERS LIVED

Early settlers built houses of logs. Families started with one-room cabins and later added another room. The roofed space left between the two rooms was called a "dog-trot" because the family dog liked to sleep there in the cool breeze.

Meals were cooked over an outside fire or in the fireplace of the cabin. Bacon and cornbread were the foods served most often. Deer, wild turkey, and other small animals were brought home by hunters as a special food treat.

Wool from sheep was spun into thread and cloth by the women settlers. They made clothes and leather shoes for all the family members. Caps were made from coonskins or woven from plants. Furry bearskins became blankets.

From the Indians, settlers learned the kinds of plants to use as medicines. Indians also taught them how to soften deerskins and sew them into jackets, trousers, and moccasins.

14

SOME EARLY TEXAS LEADERS
GAIL BORDEN

Gail Borden came to San Felipe in 1830. He started a newspaper called "Telegraph and Texas Register". It was the first successful newspaper in the colony.

Gail Borden was also a surveyor and an inventor. He discovered how to make canned milk and dried foods that would not spoil. However, it was many years before people began to use his inventions.

LOUIS BERLANDIER

In Europe, scientists wanted to learn about the plants and animals of Texas. They sent men called NATURALISTS to study the things of Nature—birds, plants, animals, and insects, as well as shells, rocks, and the land itself.

Louis Berlandier, a Frenchman, came to Texas in 1828. He was the first person to send drawings and samples of plants and animals back to scientists in Europe. They put this information about Texas into books and museums.

WILLIAM GOYENS

William Goyens was the son of a freed slave who came to Nacogdoches. He worked as a blacksmith who made wagons and guns. Goyens hauled freight and ran an inn, a gristmill, and a sawmill. Because he spoke several Indian languages, he was appointed as an agent to work with the Indians around Nacogdoches. William Goyens became well known as a leader in early Texas.

MEXICO CHANGES ITS MIND

Mexico saw that Texas was being filled with great numbers of Anglos from the United States. It was afraid that Texas would soon want to belong to the United States instead of Mexico. So the rulers said that no more Anglos could come into Texas. This made the colonists unhappy. They asked the rulers to let them take part in making laws for Texas. But Mexico would not listen to them.

18

In 1832, leaders came from all the colonies to meet in San Felipe. They chose Stephen Austin to go to Mexico City to ask once again for better laws. He went in 1833 but could not see the rulers because many people were ill from a plague of cholera.

After many months, the sickness passed. When the Mexican officials were able to talk to Mr. Austin, they promised to make better laws for Texas.

On his way home, Austin was suddenly arrested at Saltillo and taken to a jail in Mexico City. He was kept in jail for almost a year because the Mexican rulers were afraid he was planning for Texas to free itself from Mexico.

The SETTLERS TALK OF FREEDOM

At last, Stephen Austin was allowed to leave the jail and return to Texas. He had been gone for 2½ years. The colonists greeted him with great joy. But they were angry with Mexico. They talked often about revolting from the rule of Mexico.

Sam Houston, a lawyer from Nacogdoches, was one of the new leaders in favor of being free from Mexico. He wanted Texas to be a part of the United States.

Anahuac

The president of Mexico was determined that Texas would remain a part of Mexico. He sent soldiers to live in Texas towns and told them to take away the guns of the settlers. He made the settlers pay taxes to support the soldiers.

This made the Texans angry enough to fight. In the town of Anahuac, William Travis led some Texans to capture 40 Mexican troops in June, 1835. Although the fight did not last long, it has sometimes been called the first battle of the Texas Revolution against Mexico.

The FIGHT at GONZALES—1835

In the town of Gonzales, another short battle took place in October 1835. When 180 Mexican soldiers came to take the town's only cannon, a crowd of Texans stood around it. They held a flag which said "Come and Take It". When the Mexican soldiers could not capture the cannon, they left Gonzales.

TEXAS DECLARES ITS INDEPENDENCE— 1836

WASHINGTON-ON-THE-BRAZOS

On March 1, 1836, leaders of the colonists met in the tiny town of Washington, a town on the Brazos River. In a cold, drafty blacksmith shop, they all signed a Declaration of Independence. They agreed to fight Mexico so that Texas would be free.

Sam Houston became the Commander-in-Chief of the Texans and began to gather soldiers for a Texas army. Stephen Austin went to New York to borrow money from the United States to pay the soldiers and to buy guns and supplies.

The BATTLE at the ALAMO—March 6, 1836

Santa Anna came from Mexico with a large army. He marched his men to San Antonio where a few Texas soldiers were in the Alamo fort.

William Travis, commander of the Texans at the Alamo, knew that his men were far outnumbered by Mexican troops. But he and the Texans stayed to fight, saying they would never give up.

After a battle of 13 days, all the Texans were lost. Santa Anna's troops climbed the walls of the fort and overwhelmed them.

Near the town of Goliad, the Texans lost another battle with the Mexicans on March 20, 1836.

The RETREAT

Santa Anna and his men marched into East Texas to hunt for Sam Houston and his little army. For 6 weeks, the Texans hid from Santa Anna. As they hurried through the countryside, General Houston ordered the towns of San Felipe and Gonzales to be burned. The Texans did not want the Mexican army to be able to use the houses or the food stored in the towns.

San Jacinto

The BATTLE of SAN JACINTO—April 21, 1836

General Houston trained the Texas men to be better soldiers. He wanted them to be ready to attack the Mexicans at the right time.

Finally, on April 21, 1836, Texan scouts reported that the Mexican soldiers were resting in a meadow at San Jacinto. General Houston and his men were nearby. He ordered the Texans to rush upon the Mexicans. Shouting "Remember the Alamo!" and "Remember Goliad!," they won the battle in less than 20 minutes because the Mexicans were not prepared to fight. Santa Anna was captured. He promised to allow Texas to be free from Mexican rule. He also promised to take all of his army out of Texas and not to fight again.

The REPUBLIC of TEXAS

After the Battle of San Jacinto, Texas became a country which ruled itself. It was called the REPUBLIC of TEXAS. Sam Houston was elected as the first president. Senators and Representatives were chosen to make laws for the new country.

Columbia

The town of Columbia was chosen to be the first capital of the Republic. The lawmakers met there in two small houses to work out the problems of the new country. They worked to plan ways to pay off war debts, to make peace with the Indians, and to make a prosperous life for the people of Texas.

They also chose a flag which held a Lone Star, and wide red, white, and blue stripes. For the next ten years, this flag flew over the new country . . . the Republic of Texas.

CAN YOU REMEMBER?

1. Who owned Texas when Stephen Austin brought settlers? ______
______
2. What kinds of trouble did the first settlers have? ______
______
3. How did Baron von Bastrop help the colonists? ______
4. What was the name of the first town built by Anglos? ______
5. What is a "dog-trot" cabin? ______
6. Who was William Goyens? ______
7. Why did Mexico stop Anglo settlers from coming into Texas?
______
______
8. Why did the colonists revolt from Mexico? ______
______
9. What happened at the Alamo? ______
10. What happened to Texas after the Battle of San Jacinto? ______
______

WHAT CAME FIRST?

Use the numbers 1, 2, 3, 4, 5, to show which event happened first.

____ Anglo settlers built the town of San Felipe.
____ Santa Anna won the battle at the Alamo.
____ Mexico won its freedom from Spain.
____ Stephen F. Austin brought settlers from the United States.
____ After the Battle of San Jacinto, Texas became a Republic.

MAKE THEM MATCH
Draw a line from the word to the picture that matches it.

dog-trot cabin

deer

Mexican flag

the Alamo

peace pipe

cannon

surveyor

coonskin cap

cotton

Lone Star flag

IS IT TRUE?

Write a T before each sentence which is true.

1. _____ Santa Anna was a Mexican general.

2. _____ Stephen Austin brought Anglo settlers to Texas.

3. _____ Early settlers built brick houses.

4. _____ Baron von Bastrop was a railroad engineer.

5. _____ Settlers named the first town San Felipe de Austin.

6. _____ Gail Borden invented ice-cream.

7. _____ William Goyens was the first resident of Texas.

8. _____ Sam Houston led the Texans to victory at the Battle of San Jacinto.